# INSIDE BIOSPHERE 2

## Earth Science Under Glass

*by* **Mary Kay Carson**  *with photographs by* **Tom Uhlman**

HOUGHTON MIFFLIN HARCOURT
BOSTON   NEW YORK

The text was set in Plantin Standard.

The Library of Congress Catalog has cataloged the hardcover edition as follows:
Carson, Mary Kay, author.
  Inside Biosphere 2 : earth science under glass / by Mary Kay Carson ; with photographs by Tom Uhlman.
     pages cm
  Audience: Ages 10+
  Audience: Grades 7 to 8
  1. Biosphere 2 (Project)—Juvenile literature. 2. Closed ecological systems (Space environment)—Juvenile literature. 3. Human ecology—Juvenile literature. 4. Ecology—Research—Juvenile literature. I. Uhlman, Tom, illustrator. II. Title. III. Title: Inside Biosphere Two.
  TL1500.C37 2015
  304.2—dc23
                    2014047046

ISBN: 978-0-544-41664-2 hardcover
ISBN: 978-0-358-36258-6 paperback

Manufactured in China
SCP 10 9 8 7 6 5 4 3 2 1
4500824032

# CONTENTS

The Biosphere 2 scientist Joost van Haren checks the branch bag to make sure it's sealed up tight.

# INDOOR NATURE TOUR

he air is warm, humid, and smells green. Towering trees stand trunk to trunk, their leafy crowns letting in only a few thin shafts of sunlight. Near the ground the forest is especially dim and damp. Leaves of many shapes and sizes litter a slippery pathway, and noodle-like roots dangle at eye level from overhead vines. Up ahead in the rainforest is a cliffy mound of dark rock with a tall man standing on top of it. He's holding a leafy tree branch. The man gently fits the leaves inside a squarish, clear plastic bag without detaching them from the branch. The man expertly seals the bag. "That's why it's called a branch bag," says the smiling scientist in a crisp Dutch accent. A black tube attaches to the bag and shuttles air into it. Soon it's inflated like a small see-through pillow. Why wrap leaves in an air-filled bag? The scientist wants to know what happens as the leaves soak up carbon dioxide. "We are tracking where the carbon goes," he says.

A loud, mechanical squawk interrupts the explanation. Then a cheery voice booms through the trees. "That's Joost van Haren, folks! He's our rainforest scientist!" says a tour guide through a microphone. Its speaker makes a second painful squawk. "Say hi to Joost, everybody!" Tourists in shorts and flip-flops wave from a wooden deck above the far end of the wet pathway. "Hallow," says Joost with a quick salute. Just above the T-shirted onlookers, bits of blue sky crisscrossed with white bars peek through the greenery. A framework of white steel triangles holds countless windows.

Not much light reaches the ground in a rainforest.

## "We are tracking where the carbon goes."

This rainforest isn't in the Amazon or Asia. It's inside a gigantic greenhouse in the Arizona desert. This is Biosphere 2, an enormous, enclosed research facility. It's larger than three acres. There's more than rainforest under its glass roofs. There's also an ocean, a savannah, and three huge hillsides of newborn soil.

Experiments and research happen in Biosphere 2's rainforest and other areas that couldn't take place anywhere else. It has spaces big enough to support complex ecosystems similar to those in nature. But Biosphere 2 is indoors, so scientists can carefully control conditions for experiments and are able to make repeated, precise measurements over time.

Biosphere 2 is a bridge between a laboratory and the real world. It's a place where scientists can study how our living planet is changing. And it's open to the public. Visitors come to witness the environmental research at Biosphere 2, learn how it was built, and find out what happened twenty-five years ago when eight human beings sealed themselves inside it for two long years.

The location for Biosphere 2 was chosen for its high number of sunny days. The biospherians wanted lots of sunlight to grow food.

The air inside the giant greenhouse expands as it warms, putting constant pressure on the glass panels. To keep them from popping out, Biosphere 2's builders gave it two "lungs." The lungs are large domes the size of ice rinks, each with a flexible rubber ceiling that rises as the pressure inside Biosphere 2 increases, and sags as the temperature cools.

# CHAPTER 1

# SPACESHIP EARTH

Biosphere 2 was quite a scene on the morning of September 26, 1991. Thousands of people crowded on the lawn outside the structure's Human Habitat building. News photographers, reporters, and camera crews swarmed near a metal door that resembled a submarine hatch. It was Biosphere 2's air lock. Eight people dressed in identical dark blue jumpsuits were

Biospherians (left to right) Abigail Alling, Roy Walford, Jane Poynter, Taber MacCallum, Linda Leigh, Mark Nelson, Sally Silverstone, and Mark Van Thillo walk through the air lock on September 26, 1991.

the center of everyone's attention. Each took a turn at a microphone, saying a few words. Television helicopters flew over Biosphere 2, skimming by its gleaming pyramid, glass triple arches, and dome-topped library tower. Then at eight o'clock the eight biospherians, as they were called, entered the air lock. They stepped through the metal hatch and, with a clang, swung it shut behind them. The four men and four women would not come out for 730 days.

It was an experiment in human survival, and the biospherians were the lab rats.

### A BOTTLED-UP MINI EARTH

The goal of Biosphere 2's creators was to build an enclosed living environment that could provide humans with all of their needed air, water, and food. Why? To prove that it could be done, and that they were smart enough to do it. The project's funders also wanted to invent and sell technologies for living in space stations and on other planets, like Mars.

The model for Biosphere 2 was Earth's biosphere, or what they called Biosphere 1. The biosphere is our planet's living layer. It's where air, sunlight, water, and soil interact to support life in its millions of forms. Seeing our planet from space starkly illustrates how separate and self-contained it is. Earth is a closed system. All of our biosphere's air, water, and rocks are contained within that blue sphere with nothing but dark, cold space surrounding it. Biosphere 2 was built as a closed system too. It was sealed shut so no air, water, or anything else could come in. Like with Earth, only sunlight entered. Nothing could get out of Biosphere 2, either. Once the door shut, whatever wastes and gases were created stayed inside. Water swirling down drains didn't flow into city sewers. It was cleaned and reused. That's why bathrooms had handheld water sprayers instead of toilet paper, which would get in the way of recycling the water. The carbon dioxide we exhale and pol-lutants from everyday things such as glue and dyes continually go into our air. Toxic wastes like these are diluted in Earth's atmosphere, but quickly become concentrated in the limited air inside of Biosphere 2.

The idea was to set up an ecosystem with plants, animals, and a working water cycle. Once up and running, the system was designed to keep going by itself. Planet Earth does this all the time. Plants clean the air and make oxygen, marshes purify water, and sunlight fuels plants to make food. The bio-spherians were meant to survive inside the sealed environment by breathing oxygen made by plants, composting all leftovers and leavings (including human waste), growing food, and re-cycling water.

**Biosphere 2's rainforest is inside its stout glass pyramid, seen on the left here.**

Biosphere 2 was built as a miniature Earth, complete with five miniature wilderness biomes: an ocean with a coral reef and coconut palm beach; a rainforest with three hundred different kinds of plants and a waterfall; a fog desert with cacti and succulents adapted to dry soil but moist air; a savannah including grassland and an orchard; and a mangrove wetland with water-filtering plants and fish.

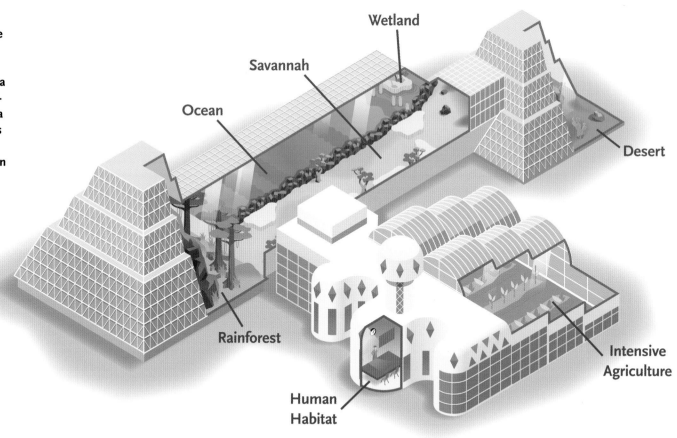

Wetland

Savannah

Ocean

Desert

Rainforest

Intensive Agriculture

Human Habitat

# BIOSPHERE 2 FACTS & STATS

Biosphere 2 is a spectacular structure. Here are some of the details of what went into building it:

- 3.14 acres (1.27 hectares) under glass

- 7.2 million cubic feet (203,900 cubic meters) under sealed glass

- 6,600 windows, each made of two glass panes joined by a layer of strong plastic

- 73,000 steel supports, or struts, to make up the frame

- 22 miles (35.4 kilometers) of caulk to seal windows to frame

- 500-ton (454-metric-ton) liner of stainless steel to line the ground

- 91 feet (27.7 meters) tall at highest point

- $150–$250 million in private money paid by the Texas billionaire Ed Bass

- 4 years to build (1987–1991)

- Constructed to last 100 years

Biosphere 2 was constructed with more than 70,000 white-painted steel supports, or struts, that hold some 6,600 windows.

Cleaning, maintaining, and repairing the highest of Biosphere 2's windows requires climbing gear. Isabel Stubblefield uses ropes and a harness for her job maintaining the structure. She's worked at Biosphere 2 for twenty-five years.

## A TEMPLE TO ENGINEERING

Biosphere 2 is a true engineering achievement. Thousands of glass windows attach to a triangular frame of steel supports, or struts. The entire 3.14-acre (1.27-hectare) structure sits on a slab of stainless steel, like a cookie sheet the size of three football fields. This seals it off from the ground below. When construction ended, Biosphere 2 was the world's most airtight structure. It leaked less air than the space shuttle!

Biosphere 2 was built with what was called a Human Habitat, as well. There were apartments, a kitchen, labs, and

The glass used in the windows blocks out about half the sun's energy, including UV light. You can't get sunburned inside Biosphere 2.

Inside the dome at the top of the 87-foot (26.5-meter) tower is a library where the biospherians could read and relax, if they had the energy to climb the spiral staircase to get up there.

meeting rooms, along with a half-acre (2,000-square-meter) farming area where the biospherians gardened and raised chickens, pigs, and goats to eat. The ocean, desert, savannah, rainforest, and mangrove wetland were called wilderness biomes. They provided life support by making oxygen, cleaning water, and soaking up carbon dioxide. While natural ecosystems were meant to support the biospherians, technology provided the conditions those ecosystems need. Biosphere 2's weather—temperature, humidity, wind, and rain—is created by machines housed in its enormous basement and powered by its Energy Center. Temperatures inside Biosphere 2 on a summer day without electric-powered air conditioning would get hot enough to damage plants within twenty minutes.

"[Biosphere 2] would be a great place to look at Earth system processes, and that's what it is today."

### HUNGRY FOR ADVENTURE

The eight biospherians were scientists, engineers, and a doctor. But they had trained to also become plumbers, farmers, electricians, and water treatment experts. The biospherians grew their own food, ran all of the equipment, and continually monitored all the weather conditions and levels of gases inside. The biospherians worked long hours, often at backbreaking chores. And they didn't sit down to big meals after a day of work. Growing enough food turned out to be harder than

Mark Nelson and Jane Poynter dish up some supper in the dining room during the 1991–1993 mission. All of the biospherians' food was grown inside the giant greenhouse.

Taber MacCallum, Abigail Alling, and Linda Leigh take a coffee break during the 1991–1993 mission.

expected. The weather during the two-year mission was unusually cloudy because of El Niño, so sunlight was decreased. Some crops didn't grow well, and plant diseases and pests took a toll too. Most of the time each biospherian ate only about 1,780 calories per day. That's not much more than a fast food hamburger meal. Skimpy harvests weren't the only surprise. Correctly accounting for all the oxygen and carbon dioxide inside the sealed greenhouse was another problem. By the start of year two, the biospherians were living in air with an oxygen level equivalent to the top of a 15,000-foot (4,572-meter) mountain.

"After thirteen months in Biosphere 2, we were starving, suffocating, and going quite mad," wrote the biospherian Jane Poynter. Breathing became so difficult that a year and a half into their two-year mission, the seal was broken to add oxygen to Biosphere 2's air. For some, this meant failure. Feuding and fighting among the biospherians piled on stress too, but all eight remained inside for the two entire years. When the crew exited through the same hatch in 1993, most looked tired, thin, and relieved to be out.

## NEW OWNERS, NEW PURPOSE

Was the two-year mission a failure? Not if it was an experiment and the goal was new knowledge. The trouble with carbon dioxide and oxygen levels actually led to Biosphere 2's future success. A scientific paper written about the problem got many scientists thinking about Biosphere 2 as a really big laboratory. "It seeded the idea that it would be a great place to look at Earth system processes," explains Biosphere 2's current deputy director, John Adams, "and that's what it is today."

No one lives inside the Human Habitat or grows their dinner under the arches of glass. Twenty-first-century Biosphere 2 inhabitants are researchers and students, many from the University of Arizona, which has operated Biosphere 2 since 2007. It's the research facility for the university's B2 Earthscience program and also a tourist destination. "About a

# FLASH-BACK TO THE BIOSPHERIANS

Jane Poynter and Taber MacCallum play music in the orchard. The pair got married after the mission ended in 1993. Look for other Flash-Back to the Biospherians features to learn more about how the original biospherians lived during the 1991–93 mission.

hundred thousand people come through the door every year," says John. Visitors can even walk through that famous metal air-lock hatch. Many come to satisfy their curiosity about the original biospherians, says John, "but at the same time they're really interested in how it is being used today"—such as why Biosphere 2 scientists are studying how rainforests and oceans soak up carbon dioxide, how life and water turn rock into soil, and ways to conserve energy and live greener. Twenty-five years after its construction, research at Biosphere 2 is now focused on what's happening to Earth, not how to colonize Mars. As John explains, "It's research that impacts all of our lives."

Weather stations mounted on latticed metal poles inside Biosphere 2's rainforest continually measure temperature, humidity, wind speeds, and sunlight at different levels of the forest.

# CHAPTER 2

# EXPERIMENTAL RAINFOREST

**B**ack in Biosphere 2's rainforest, Joost van Haren is still at work. He inspects a different branch bag, checking the health of the leaves inside.

A closer look around the rainforest reveals all kinds of scientific sensors, as well as wires and water pipes. Yellow plastic cylinders stick out of the dirt, catching and measuring rain created by overhead sprinklers. Poles packed with weather station instruments stand among the trees. These instruments are busy measuring wind, temperature, sunlight, and humidity. Thin black tubing snakes up rocklike walls, and gadgets peek out from behind leaves and vines. It may look like a real rainforest, but it's not.

"This is a model ecosystem," says Joost. It's a simplified forest. No chattering monkeys or parrots live in it. "But the plants in this rainforest function like any other plants," he says. They use the sun's energy to turn water and carbon dioxide into food through photosynthesis, releasing oxygen in the process. The indoor rainforest's original purpose was to produce needed oxygen for the biospherians, in the same way that forests in nature make oxygen we breathe. The leaves surrounding Joost swap gases with the air around them just as trees in the Amazon do. And because this rainforest copy is in Biosphere 2, scientists can use it to learn about real forests in ways researchers working in nature never could.

The leaves inside the branch bag continue to photosynthesize, so Joost can track the carbon dioxide they take up.

Branch bags are made of Mylar plastic. A computer fan, toy putty, a bit of flexible hose, and some weather stripping make it inflatable and airtight. A trouser hanger holds it in place.

Rain gauges capture the artificial rainfall so it can be measured.

"Biogeochemists look at how biology changes the chemistry on Earth."

## UNDER THE MAGNIFYING GLASS

Earth's atmosphere goes up for miles, including the thick layer of air above real forests. The atmosphere above Biosphere 2's rainforest stops at the 88-foot (27-meter) glass roof. "The amount of air in here is very small compared to the amount of plants, leaves, and soil," says Joost. The condensed air-and-plant mix gives scientists a zoomed-in and sped-up view of how they interact. "This rainforest is like a magnifying glass," he says. Joost is able to precisely measure gases coming and going between air, leaves, and microbes in the soil. That's where the leaf-holding branch bags come in, and all the aquarium-like tubing everywhere. Pumps pull in air through the tubes from all over the rainforest. The air is shuttled into instruments that identify and measure the gases in it. A computer logs and tracks the amounts and sources of carbon dioxide, oxygen, and water in real time. "And how the amounts

"Tropical forests store lots of carbon dioxide," says Joost. The greenhouse gas is leading to warmer overall temperatures on Earth and to global climate change.

No jaguars or toucans live in this rainforest. But there are snails and cockroaches that break down fallen leaves. Ants do most of the insect pollination.

Forests continuously exchange gases with the air around them. During sun-powered photosynthesis, leaves open their stomates to take in carbon dioxide and release the oxygen made. That's also when water escapes. Soil releases carbon dioxide as bacteria break down leaves.

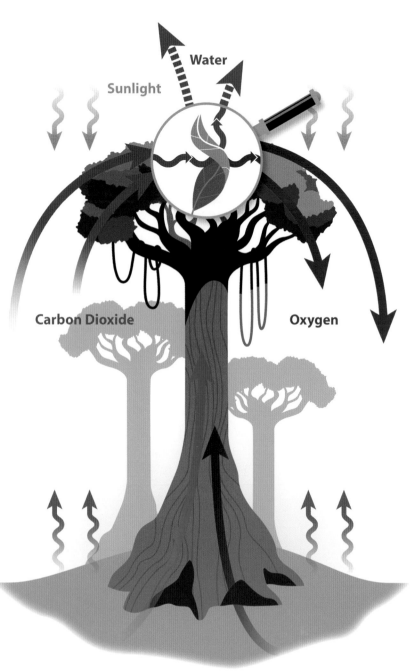

Water

Sunlight

Carbon Dioxide

Oxygen

change with different levels of precipitation, temperature, and carbon dioxide," explains Joost. A rainforest built as an oxygen factory for eight biospherians nearly three decades ago is now a big green test tube.

Joost van Haren has been working at Biosphere 2 since not long after the biospherians moved out. He's seen its rainforest grow and change for twenty years and knows every inch of it. But he's not a botanist, or plant scientist, by training. Joost began his science career studying geology in his native Netherlands. He started working at Biosphere 2 in 1995. "That's when I realized that all the rocks here are fake, so I better do something else," Joost jokes. Biosphere 2's density of plants in so little atmosphere quickly captured his curiosity. He's been studying their interactions ever since. Now Joost is a biogeochemist. "Biogeochemists look at how biology changes the chemistry on Earth," he explains—for example, how trees change the mix of gases in the atmosphere.

## OUR CHANGING GLOBE

"We use this rainforest to test what goes on in the real world," says Joost. One real-world example is how forests will handle climate change. Carbon dioxide levels in Earth's atmosphere are going up, causing the planet's overall temperature to rise too. Fossil fuel use over the past century is to blame. Coal, petroleum, and natural gas were once plants and animals full of carbon, like all living things. When we burn fossil fuels to power cars and heat homes, their carbon moves into the atmosphere as carbon dioxide gas. Plants take carbon dioxide out of the air during photosynthesis and put breathable oxygen into the air. Plants and trees take in a lot of carbon dioxide while photosynthesizing food for growth. Forests are important absorbers of carbon in Earth's atmosphere. Will future forests be able to soak up all the extra carbon dioxide we're putting into the atmosphere?

That's one of the biggest experiments in Biosphere 2's forest, says Joost. Scientists studied what happened after adding increasing amounts of carbon dioxide gas. "On the short term, the whole forest responds like a big leaf," explains Joost.

The biospherians spent three years installing the plants and building their oxygen-factory rainforest before their 1991 move-in. Today the rainforest within Biosphere 2's pyramid is a large laboratory for experiments where conditions can be changed and the results studied.

It soaks up the extra carbon dioxide, using it during photosynthesis. But not forever. After a while, the forest can't absorb any more. It has all the carbon dioxide it can use to photosynthesize food. Like a water tank that's already full, the forest becomes maxed out, and any more added carbon dioxide is overflow that stays in the air. Trees can only use and store so much carbon. Biosphere 2's forest stopped taking up carbon dioxide once its level about doubled what is in our atmosphere right now. Forests can't soak up endless amounts of carbon dioxide.

Doing the math, "In about a hundred years tropical forests aren't going to help us anymore," says Joost. Their carbon-storing space will be full. "And a real rainforest is likely going to max out sooner," he explains. Your average tropical forest doesn't have soil as rich in nutrients as Biosphere 2's soil. Poor soil limits how much food a tree can photosynthesize.

Trees and plants need water as well as nutrients. Drought is a real threat to forests. "With climate change we know that rainforests are going to get less rain," says Joost. "But what we really want to understand is what exactly drought is going to do to the ecosystem." Scientists investigating real tropical forests have worked on finding out. They've created drought conditions by setting up forest ground covers that keep rainwater from reaching the soil. These trees can still get water from rain on leaves and out of the humid air, though. Stopping rain in a rainforest is difficult. "Here in Biosphere 2 we make it rain whenever we want," says Joost. Want to create a drought? Just shut off the sprinklers and wait.

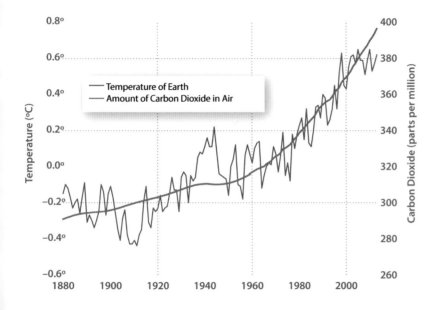

The amount of carbon dioxide in the air has increased since factories and cars began burning lots of fossil fuels a century ago. The overall average temperature on Earth has increased too.

## A NOT-SO-RAINY FOREST

Biosphere 2 has created some short droughts in the past. Now Joost is gearing up for a longer one in their rainforest. "We'll cut all the water," he says. "It won't rain for two months." Meanwhile, temperature and other conditions inside the rainforest will stay the same. That's another benefit of Biosphere 2's controllable environment. In nature, factors such as higher temperatures, windstorms, or invading pests could be adding to a drought's damage. Those other factors, or variables, aren't an issue inside Biosphere 2. Joost can focus on water and where the trees are finding it, such as in the soil or air, and how that affects their photosynthesis.

Photosynthesis happens in leaves. When tiny pores in leaves, called stomates, are open, they take in carbon dioxide from the air. A leaf with open stomates loses water, the way steam escapes out an open shower door. Leaves must balance their need for carbon dioxide with their need to hold on to water. "During a drought that balance goes out of whack," explains Joost. It tips away from making food to the water-saving side. "There are two ways trees can reduce the amount of water they lose. One is by just dropping leaves." Fewer photosynthesizing leaves with open stomates means the tree keeps more water. "Another way is for a tree to keep all its leaves," says Joost. Instead, all the leaves together cut back on taking in carbon dioxide. Their stomates stay closed more to conserve water, but each leaf will photosynthesize less, and therefore make less food and not grow as much.

Joost and other researchers monitor the different trees during droughts, checking on their photosynthesis, tracing their carbon, and tracking where they get water. There are about ninety species of trees inside Biosphere 2's rainforest.

Weather stations inside Biosphere 2's rainforest include light sensors, humidity-sensing hygrometers, thermometers, and wind-measuring anemometers.

This refrigerator-sized hole with glass walls is a soil pit. It goes all the way down to the concrete floor under the rainforest's 10 feet (3 meters) of soil. The soil pit is perfect for seeing how roots grow, and there are tubes for taking gas samples, too.

Different species react to drought differently. Whether or not trees drop leaves is measured with a lidar (light detection and ranging) device. It sits on a tripod and rotates, sending out laser light pulses that create a three-dimensional picture. It looks kind of like a weather radar image. The picture shows which parts of the forest are covered in foliage and which are open to sunlight. "You can make an incredible recreation of both the biomass and leaf area, so you know how photosynthesis is happening," says Joost. Lidar imaging will allow Joost to measure the amount of leaves dropped, showing how the forest changes during and after a long drought.

## FROM ARIZONA TO AMAZONIA

Lidar is used to image real rainforests too, including sites in Peru and Brazil where Joost has done field studies. Biosphere 2 is a great place for trying out research equipment. "We can test it out here in conditions that are close to the rainforest," says Joost. He and others in Biosphere 2 use the same tree-climbing ropes and gear that researchers in the Amazon use. How else could they reach the highest treetops? Seeing how the upper level leaves photosynthesize is important because it's where most of the sunlight is, just like in a real rainforest. Unlike in nature, this rainforest has a ceiling that traps rising hot air, making temperatures increase with height. "So the highest leaves will be more greatly affected by the drought," says Joost.

Discoveries made in Biosphere 2's rainforest are being put to use in the field, too. Joost explains that they've measured VOCs (volatile organic compounds) given off by Biosphere 2's trees. VOCs are unstable chemicals that readily vaporize into

Joost checks on a branch bag near a weather station to make sure the leaves are healthy.

Microbes in soil change the mix of gases in the air. There are more than twenty soil chambers like this one inside Biosphere 2's rainforest. Air pulled out of the chambers is analyzed for carbon dioxide made by microbes in the soil. Five of the rainforest soil chambers are automated. They have self-closing lids that shut for six minutes so the rate of carbon dioxide buildup can be measured.

the air and react with other gases. VOCs have a bad reputation because some are toxic chemicals found in smelly paint, glues, and cleaners. However, plants and trees naturally produce some of these unstable gases too. Because trees release only small amounts of VOCs, and not all the time, the compounds are hard for scientists to detect in nature. But it's easier to find them in Biosphere 2's rainforest because of the magnifying effect of its limited air. It's like looking for a needle in a pile of grass instead of a whole haystack. While figuring out methods of sampling the air around trees to best detect and track VOCs inside Biosphere 2's rainforest, researchers made an interesting discovery. The trees spewed the most VOCs when under stress, such as during dry seasons. Once researchers knew how to look, they found the same VOCs in real rainforests too. Joost says VOCs are a useful gauge of drought stress.

Joost also uses findings by field researchers inside Biosphere 2's rainforest. For example, researchers in the field are reporting that drought-stricken trees are growing thinner, finer roots. Thin roots can more easily reach into those last damp nooks and crannies. Changes in root size are now something Joost looks for in the Biosphere 2 drought experiments.

## TWENTY-SECOND-CENTURY FORESTS

Predicting the future of tropical forests is a big part of rainforest research these days. Forests affect climate, and climate change will affect forests. Computer models run equations and crunch data to come up with predictions of Earth's future temperatures, rainfall amounts, and sea levels. Biosphere 2 can help make climate-predicting models more accurate. "We can measure changes particularly well here that are very dif-

The computer and electronic equipment inside this small shack operates the system of pumps and valves that shuttles air into an analyzer and records the results. "It's not very tidy, but it works!" says Joost.

ficult to do in the real world," explains Joost. Data collected in the indoor forest about temperatures and carbon dioxide levels gets put into the computer models to test them. "We see how we need to adjust the computer models that people use to model the real rainforest," explains Joost.

After all, the rainforest in Biosphere 2 is already battle-tested for a warmer world. It's 9–18°F (5–10°C) hotter than an average tropical forest. Not all the species planted by the biospherians have survived the heat over the decades. "We know that in the real world temperatures are going to increase as well," says Joost. "So is this the tropical forest of the twenty-second century? This might be what it looks like." Joost wants

this green, muggy rainforest-mimic to help scientists find out. "Biosphere 2 by itself is a beautiful greenhouse and great for experimentation," he says. "But it's only useful if the findings are confirmed in the real world."

# FLASH-BACK
## TO THE BIOSPHERIANS

Eight humans weren't the only primates sealed in Biosphere 2 for two years. Four African bush babies, or galagos, accompanied the biospherians during their time inside. The biospherians named them (Topaz, Opal, Oxide, and William Kim), fed them monkey chow, and watched as they learned to climb the metal frames surrounding the glass. The nocturnal primates are tree-dwellers, so they spent a lot of time in the rainforest and orchard, snacking on fruit. The galagos were mating pairs, and two babies were born inside Biosphere 2. The biospherians could hear their territorial calls at night echoing across the wilderness biomes.

The marine biologist and Biosphere 2 scientist Rafe Sagarin paddles across the B2 ocean. The small beach at the far end sits below a stone wall. The rainforest lies beyond and above it.

# CHAPTER 3
# OCEAN WITH DESERT DREAMS

A man paddles through the water near a beach shaded in palm trees. Stone steps lead up from the sand to what looks like part of a vine-covered ancient ruin. The boat is only a few yards offshore. It's a small craft, but the waves are gentle and the man with dark curly hair steers it with confidence. As a marine biologist, Rafe Sagarin has spent a lot of time on boats. He heads away from the small beach, paddling toward a rocky cliff where a dock awaits. At Rafe's back is a wall of glass and white steel supports that slopes up and over the small sea. This is the B2 ocean, a giant saltwater tank inside Biosphere 2. Rafe Sagarin has big plans for it. "We want to transform this 700,000-gallon [2,650,000-liter] tank into something that looks like the Gulf of California," he says.

## A CHALLENGING ECOSYSTEM

Biosphere 2's builders modeled the indoor ocean after a tropical coral reef. They shipped in sand from the Bahamas and brought in fish, sea stars, sea urchins, lobsters, and living coral from the Caribbean. A convoy of milk trucks hauled in seawater from the Pacific Ocean. Living corals need moving water, so builders installed a wave machine that continually swished seawater over the corals. Tropical reefs have warm water year-round, as does the B2 ocean. "It's been kept at a temperature range of 72 to 78 degrees Fahrenheit [23°C to 25.5°C]," says Rafe. It takes a lot of electricity to heat all that water, plus run the wave machine, pumps, and water filters. The ocean is the biggest energy hog in Biosphere 2. And it's also no longer a living coral reef.

> "The Gulf of California is an amazing place, one of the most biologically rich environments on Earth."

Trouble began back in the time of the original biospherians, who soon learned that an interconnected ocean ecosystem isn't an easy thing to recreate. A surprise clan of octopuses had stowed away in the rocky coral and ate up many of the marine creatures. Weeding out the overgrowing algae was a continual chore. The glass windows over the ocean

Rafe tells visitors, "You just walked out of the desert and now you're looking at an ocean that's connected to the desert."

also blocked out too much sunlight for the corals to thrive. Eventually the corals died and the algae took over. The underground viewing windows in the oceanview gallery become covered with the green stuff within weeks of being cleaned. Twenty-five years later, fish still live in the B2 ocean, though there are fewer and not as many kinds. It's still an ecosystem— the fish aren't fed by humans—but not a terribly healthy or biodiverse one. This is one reason why the B2 ocean is being renovated. It's why Rafe Sagarin came to Biosphere 2.

## THE SCIENCE OF PAST LIVES

"I'm a marine ecologist," says Rafe. The sea has enchanted him most of his life. Rafe spent summers as a kid on Cape Cod, exploring the Atlantic Coast; watching the underwater explorer Jacques Cousteau's television show sealed the deal. The Pacific Ocean's rocky shores and colorful tide pools cap-

ture his interest these days, especially those that rim the Sea of Cortez, also known as the Gulf of California. It's the bit of Pacific Ocean sandwiched between mainland Mexico and its Baja peninsula. "The Gulf of California is an amazing place, one of the most biologically rich environments on Earth," says Rafe. "It's full of species of fish and invertebrates, reptiles and mammals found nowhere else."

The Gulf of California is where Rafe does his research. "I mostly study what's called historical ecology," he explains. Rafe uses historical evidence to study where marine animals once lived. "A lot of my work uses old records of what was living somewhere . . . to see how things have changed," Rafe

The B2 oceanview gallery has displays about the Gulf of California, the animals that live there, and the region's history. "The problems we see in the Gulf are problems that are all over the world's oceans," says Rafe. Water pollution, dumped plastics and trash, overfishing, and coastal developmental are global ocean challenges.

The Gulf of California, or Sea of Cortez, is home to marine mammals, fish, invertebrates, and birds of many kinds.

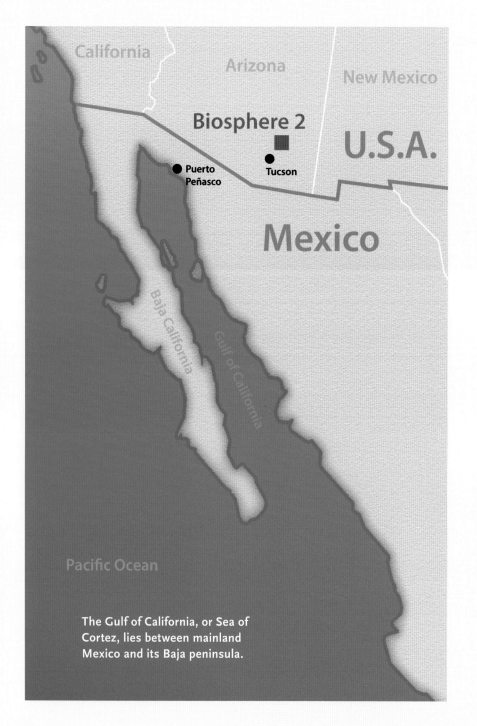

The Gulf of California, or Sea of Cortez, lies between mainland Mexico and its Baja peninsula.

says. For example, Rafe has studied century-old snail shell collections at a natural history museum. "I look at the sizes of shells from a particular location and then go back to those locations," he explains. Usually he finds smaller snails living there today. "The large ones are mostly taken by people for food." There's a link between snail size and human populations.

## FROM TROPICAL REEF TO DESERT SEA

Now Rafe is trying to explain a different kind of link to Biosphere 2's visitors, one between what they see inside and outside its glass walls: the surprising connection between the desert and sea. "The Gulf of California is the closest ocean to the Sonoran desert that surrounds Biosphere 2," says Rafe. "In fact the Sonoran desert and the Gulf couldn't exist without one another." The view outside the windows above the B2 ocean isn't of a barren landscape. The Sonoran desert is full of life, from giant cacti and mesquite trees to hawks and piglike javelinas. This desert's rich diversity comes from its monsoon weather, storms that deliver rain in late summer. Much of the monsoons' life-giving water comes up from the Gulf of California, says Rafe. Without it, Sonoran desert life wouldn't be as abundant. As Rafe points out, "You can see some of the same species of plants on the shores of the Gulf of California as you can here in the Sonoran Desert."

The B2 ocean is being repurposed as a replica of the Gulf of California to educate visitors and school groups. A Gulf-style cactus-studded island is planned for the center of the B2 ocean to immediately show the connection between desert

The Sonoran Desert surrounding
Biosphere 2 is home to more than
a hundred kinds of cacti, including
this spine-covered cholla.

Southern Arizona middle and high school students learn marine biology techniques such as water sampling and species identification while visiting Biosphere 2.

Franklin Lane (wearing cap) shows students some sampling techniques in the marine biology lab. He is an education specialist for Biosphere 2, which is visited by more than ten thousand students each year.

and sea, says Rafe. "We'll build rocky shores where researchers can study coastal organisms and teach people about how marine biologists do their work." Aquarium experts and scientists on both sides of the United States and Mexico border are helping decide which kinds of marine and coastal plants and animals are suited to life in a desert sea under glass. Water temperature is also set to change to be more like the Gulf of California. Allowing temperatures to fluctuate more naturally should help tame the B2 ocean's energy appetite, too.

The underground oceanview gallery where visitors can see into the ocean illustrates what the Sea of Cortez and the B2 ocean have in common. Both had a bountiful past full of biodiversity. Decades ago, the Gulf of California was full of tuna and other large fish, sea turtles, and whales. Overfishing, pollution, and development on the coast have changed all that. Today the Gulf, like the B2 ocean, is not in great shape. But people are working on bringing it back. They are protecting native species and fighting pollution. The B2 ocean's path is brighter too, as it's transformed into a desert sea full of life and purpose.

## AN OCEAN OF SCIENCE

B2 ocean's underground viewing windows go all the way to its rocky seafloor. Visitors watch neon-yellow fish swim by and the churning of artificial waves. Sometimes a surprise shows up. A sudden swoosh of bubbles announces a diver jumping into the tank. He kicks his finned feet, circles around, and then

This bright red popeye catalufa is one of the Gulf of California fish species on display in the B2 oceanview gallery.

Divers will be training and undergoing certification in the B2 ocean. "It's also going to be a great spot for scuba diving," says Rafe.

turns toward the glass and waves. It's Rafe. Scientists have been experimenting in the small sea under glass since soon after the biospherians left. Rafe says that the B2 ocean, like all of Biosphere 2, is a middle ground between the field and the laboratory. "It has this sweet spot between the complexity of nature and the control of the laboratory," explains Rafe.

A famous B2 ocean experiment helped to wake the world to a troubling truth: the ocean is getting more acidic. An increased amount of carbon dioxide in the air isn't just warming the planet. It's also adding acid to the ocean. When carbon dioxide and water mix they make carbonic acid. In seawater this acid reacts with calcium carbonate minerals, and these minerals are what marine creatures, such as clams and corals, use to build shells. The acid changes the minerals, mak-

Rafe Sagarin is transforming the B2 ocean into a Sea of Cortez replica.

ing them less usable for shell building. Scientists showed how this happens at Biosphere 2 by adding carbon dioxide to the B2 ocean. This acidified the seawater and changed its minerals, and with fewer construction minerals available, the corals grew smaller and more slowly overall. Ocean acidification is now a well-known threat to ocean ecosystems, especially coral reefs. The path to discovering this global problem started in Biosphere 2's indoor sea.

## A DESERT SEA LAB

More recently, University of Arizona scientists have been studying the marine microbes in the B2 ocean to develop techniques to do the same in the wild. Scientists are studying ocean bacteria, viruses, and other microbes because they affect and change seawater, sea life, and the atmosphere. Another B2 ocean research project focused on what happens to plastic trash that pollutes the ocean. "There are new bacte-

Biosphere 2's ocean is under the low rectangular glass section just behind the rainforest's pyramid.

Rafe studies turbo snails like this one. They live in the Gulf of California and eat algae.

ria that eat plastic," explains Rafe. "That's something we can study in an ocean of this size."

The B2 ocean isn't a big sterile tub or simple swimming pool; it has rocks and crevices, shadows and algae, like a real ocean. That makes it perfect for testing marine sensors and equipment. "We're going to have engineering students designing and testing remote submarines here," says Rafe. In the B2 ocean they won't need to worry about sharks or losing expensive equipment.

Rafe himself is preparing to do snail growth experiments in the B2 desert sea. It'll be much better than growing snails in aquariums. The B2 ocean has waves and rocks that snails can move in and out of. "They're not just sitting in water in a tank," he explains. Having places to hide and wave-churned

water might be influencing snail growth in the real world. The B2 ocean allows for complexity without the problem of someone taking the snails home for dinner. "Transforming our ocean into a living model of the Gulf of California is going to be a big job," admits Rafe. "But that's exactly what Biosphere 2 was built to do—tackle big problems to help us understand our natural world."

# FLASH-BACK TO THE BIOSPHERIANS

The sandy beach at one end of the B2 ocean was a favorite party site for the biospherians. This photo is of a birthday feast, one of the few occasions when the biospherians could eat their fill. On the picnic party menu was salad, rice with peanuts, pork, and vegetable dishes. Dessert was banana bread, sweet potato pie, and cheesecake.

The Biosphere 2 scientist Luke Pangle turns on the sprinklers to create a rain experiment inside LEO.

# CHAPTER 4

# EARTH SCIENCE OBSERVATORY

I t's raining. People duck into a doorway as drops of water darken a concrete walk. Raindrops also fall onto three large rectangles of bare dirt. They land on the black sandy soil with a soft *plop* and puff of dust. The sunny blue sky above the glass roof casts a crisscrossed pattern of shadows on the dampening dirt. It's only raining inside, not outside. "We're ready to turn it off," a neatly dressed man wearing glasses announces over the hiss of sprinklers. This is Biosphere 2's Landscape Evolution Observatory, or LEO. "It's the world's largest laboratory-scale earth science experiment," says Luke Pangle. "There's not another experiment like this in the world." It's why the young scientist is here.

## FROM SWEET POTATOES TO SCIENCE

This half-acre sun-soaked space was where the biospherians farmed. Now it's home to three tennis-court-sized trays of soil. Each of LEO's identical soil-filled trays slopes downward, like a hill. In fact, they are artificial hillslopes, built inside this greenhouse so that scientists can track what goes in and what comes out of the soil—such as water from sprinklers.

Biosphere 2's Landscape Evolution Observatory is big science, with big goals. Other big science projects have broken the atom into its parts, looked back in time with space telescopes, or mapped the human genome. LEO aims to unlock the secrets of the water cycle and map the evolution of rock into soil.

Luke Pangle crouches as he checks sensors on one of LEO's artificially created hillslopes covered in crushed volcanic rock.

This knowledge is desperately needed right now. Soil erosion from farming, roads, and expanding cities is on the rise across the globe. Every year more fertile soil, the kind that crops can grow in, ends up in rivers and oceans. Yet scientists don't know how long it takes rock to become new, life-sustaining soil for farms, orchards, and healthy ecosystems. How water, rock, and plants influence and change one another matters. It affects the food we eat, water we drink, and air we breathe.

Luke Pangle is an earth scientist and water expert. "A hydrologist is a scientist who studies the way that water cycles through the Earth's land surface," explains Luke. That includes tracking patterns of rain and other kinds of precipitation over time and where all that water goes—how much evaporates into the atmosphere, runs off into rivers and lakes, and is stored underground. Because its life-sized hillslopes are in a laboratory, LEO scientists can precisely track how the crushed, dark rock breaks down, or weathers, from water and microbes to become living soil. Researchers are able to study the water cycle by tracking water molecules as they move between LEO's land and its enclosed air.

Not all of Biosphere 2 was suitable for continued study, like the rainforest, or able to be reimagined, like the ocean. LEO is a new project built in the space where the biospherians used to grow food. Rows of sweet potatoes, peanuts, and beans once grew under the three arched glass roofs over LEO.

"We have tried to clip out a piece of a landscape, bring it into a controlled laboratory environment, and study it more intensively than we ever could in nature," explains Luke. The sort of landscape LEO mimics is a small hilltop water-shed. A watershed is an area of land that "sheds" water from rain, snowmelt, and sometimes creeks or streams. Its water all eventually drains into the same place, often a lake or large river. LEO models a watershed that gets water only from pre-cipitation such as rain, not streams or rivers. These kinds of watersheds are often on mountaintops, like those seen in the distance out the glass walls of Biosphere 2. In fact, a sister project to LEO is on one of those very peaks. The Critical Zone Observatory (CZO) on Mount Bigelow is only about ten miles (16 kilometers) away.

The Biosphere 2 scientist Rebecca Minor collects data at the Mount Bigelow site in the mountains south of Biosphere 2.

## OUR WATERY WORLD

At 8,300 feet (2,530 meters) up, the Mount Bigelow research site is a different world from the cacti-studded desert sur-rounding Biosphere 2. It's a thick, fragrant forest of tall pine and fir trees full of chattering chipmunks and shy mule deer. The evergreen forest seems to have little in common with LEO, until you see the hillslope where a dark-haired woman is standing. The ground is not covered in bare dirt like LEO's hillslopes, but it is about the same size and steepness. Rebecca Minor takes a water bottle out of her backpack, a chilly wind blowing her long hair around. "If I poured out my water bot-tle, where would that water go?" asks Rebecca. Like rain or snow, the water soaks into the ground, runs off into streams, ends up in underground reservoirs, evaporates, or gets soaked up by plants. How much goes where is what the Biosphere 2 research specialist is helping to figure out.

Water is worth thinking about. Without it, Earth would

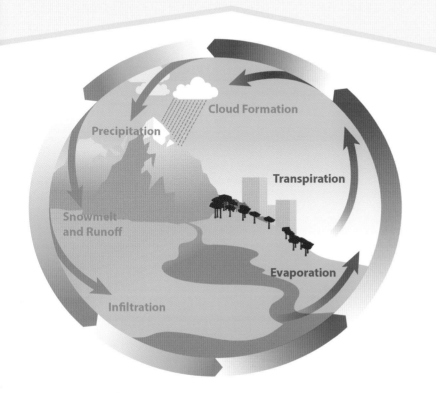

The water cycle, or hydrologic cycle, constantly moves water between Earth's land, oceans, and atmosphere.

Rain begins to fall at the Mount Bigelow CZO research site in southern Arizona's Coronado National Forest.

have no living layer, no biosphere. Water turns rock into life-supporting habitats. It releases and moves nutrients out of minerals and into plants, which become food for animals. Water cycles from falling rain and snow through soils and rivers, and evaporates back into the atmosphere. But the particulars of how much water goes where, and how quickly, aren't entirely understood.

## A BREATHING FOREST

About halfway down the forested hillslope, Rebecca kneels on ground covered in pine needles. Next to her is a gray plastic box mounted on a post. It's clicking. "That's the data logger," says Rebecca, while fishing a laptop out of her well-worn backpack. It clicks as it records information. Rebecca opens the gray box and starts hooking her laptop up to it. The box is full of electronics. "Each of these wires goes to one of the sensors in the grid," she explains. The hillslope has a buried grid of eighteen sensor sites, each marked with a slice of white PVC plastic pipe. "We have two soil moisture probes and two temperature probes at each PVC site." The sensors take moisture and temperature readings once a minute all day, every day. The plastic collars aren't just for finding the buried sensors. A soil respiration chamber, an instrument that samples the air above the soil for carbon dioxide and water vapor, fits on the collars. "It measures soil breath," says Rebecca.

While soil exhales carbon dioxide, trees and plants inhale it. Plant roots also take in water and release water vapor into the air through their leaves. Soil exhales water vapor, too, as moisture evaporates from the ground. Measuring all the gases

Weather station instruments collect temperature, humidity, and wind speeds on top of a tower at the research site.

Left: Rebecca Minor starts to download data collected by a grid of buried sensors onto her laptop. Center: This soil respiration chamber samples the air above the soil for carbon dioxide and water vapor. It fits on the PVC collars, makes a seal, and then measures the gas amounts. Right: Rebecca buried a grid of sensors like these on the hillslope at the Mount Bigelow CZO site. The pronged sensors measure soil moisture and temperature.

coming out of a mountain forest requires getting above its trees. The climb up the metal-scaffolding tower at the Mount Bigelow site ends in a chilly, breathtaking view above the treetops. The 100-foot (30-meter) tower is loaded with weather instruments, as well as little tubes that sample the air. "It's measuring carbon dioxide and water vapor from the whole ecosystem—the whole chunk of forest twenty times a second,"

says Rebecca. All the data collected is automatically logged and goes to storage electronics down at the tower's base. The tower measurements and underground soil sensor information create an overall picture of where the water goes as it moves through soil, plants, and air.

Mount Bigelow was around a long time before researchers set up their sensor grid. Like when you start a movie halfway

Rebecca checks the instruments on top of the 100-foot (30-meter) tower at the Mount Bigelow CZO site.

Both the hillslopes in LEO (top) and at the Mount Bigelow site (bottom) are small hilltop watersheds that drain water only from precipitation. No rivers or creeks flow into them.

# ZONES FOR CRITICAL SCIENCE

The Mount Bigelow research site is part of the Santa Catalina Mountains Critical Zone Observatory, or CZO. The critical zone is the layer of Earth from the tops of trees to the bottom of the groundwater. It's where rock, soil, water, air, and life interact and shape Earth's surface. The critical zone "is where life exists, where life happens," says Peter Troch, Biosphere 2 science director. "But we truly don't understand how that all works because we've always studied it from our own disciplines." A critical zone observatory is a large field research area within a watershed where scientists of many kinds study and share information among disciplines. There are ten CZOs in the United States, from Puerto Rico to Northern California. The Santa Catalina Mountains CZO is studying many of the same questions as LEO, but out in nature. Scientists are investigating the ways in which climate, rocks, soil, and wildfire affect how the critical zone changes and functions at different elevations up and down the mountain.

through, it's hard to know what's already happened. This forest has seen centuries of fires, microbes, pests, droughts, and air pollution. "And we don't really know that whole history," says Rebecca. "But with LEO, there is no evolutionary history." LEO scientists have been there from the beginning. They built a network of sensors and then added crushed rock to create a hillslope. It's simpler and more controlled, so causes and effects are easier to identity and measure. For example, after a rain shower in nature, scientists detect changes in carbon dioxide levels in the air above hillslopes. Why? In the real world there are many possible explanations, including no-longer-thirsty plants photosynthesizing and soaking up more carbon dioxide, or the soil absorbing the gas. But when carbon dioxide drops after rain has fallen on LEO's bare dirt, you know it's happening in the soil, because that's all there is. "That's the beauty of LEO," says Rebecca.

## BACK AT LAB LEO

The rain inside LEO is ending back at Biosphere 2. The sprinklers are off. Metal poles connected to the white triangular roof supports slowly unfold back into position, again hanging down over the dark dirt of the artificial watersheds. Each pole, or mast, is a weather station, complete with an anemometer for measuring wind, temperature, and humidity sensors, and a device that measures sunlight. "These allow us to monitor the climate above the LEO hillslopes," explains Luke Pangle. Each of the five masts is also equipped with tubing that sucks in air samples at five different heights. "Each one of the tubes is 200 feet [61 meters] long, so it's been a real chore for us to get all the cable and tubing up there." Luke and the

# LEO FACTS & STATS

The Landscape Evolution Observatory is a first-of-its-kind instrument and a marvel of engineering.

**Each of the three artificial watershed hillslopes**

◗ is an exact replicate for scientific accuracy

◗ sits on built-in scales that continually weigh it

◗ is 40 feet (11 meters) wide by 100 feet (30 meters) long

◗ holds 3 feet (1 meter) of crushed volcanic rock

◗ weighs 1 million pounds (454 metric tons) dry, more when soil is wet

◗ has more than 1,700 buried sensors and samplers

◗ has five suspended weather stations with air samplers

◗ will eventually be seeded with heat- and drought-resistant plants

**Construction of LEO**

◗ took five years, as long as the entire original Biosphere 2

◗ was like building three ships in a bottle, the bottle being Biosphere 2's

old agricultural area under three glass arches. Trucks carrying in steel beams to construct the hillslopes had to squeeze through a 10-by-15-foot (3-by-4.5-meter) doorway.

◗ included a "personnel transporter" moving basket suspended by a crane over each hillslope.

Poles suspended over each hillslope hold weather-measuring instruments and air-collection tubes.

The Mount Bigelow CZO site is in the Santa Catalina Mountains (visible in the background above), about 10 miles (16 kilometers) south of Biosphere 2.

More than 1,700 sensors like these are buried in LEO's hillslopes.

The big science questions of the world's biggest earth science experiment are

▶ How do water, energy, and carbon move through landscapes?

▶ How do plants and microbes change landscapes?

▶ How will climate change affect and alter sources of water?

▶ How will Earth's landscapes be reshaped by climate change?

LEO scientists can track exactly what's happening during and after a rain.

LEO team have to use ropes hanging from ceiling supports and climbing gear to install the tubing onto the weather station poles.

Getting the air sampling tubing up onto the poles has been worth it, says Luke. "It lets us monitor the carbon dioxide and water vapor leaving the hillslope and going into the atmosphere," he explains. "And how the concentrations of gases change from the soil surface all the way up to the roof 30 feet (9 meters) above." Underneath the dark dirt are hundreds of sensors that measure soil moisture, water flow, and gases at different depths, too. All the information, including continual measurements of the hillslope's weight, is shuttled to data loggers that feed into computers. "That's our automated data collection system," says Luke. "Then we have other types of instruments that we sample manually." To see those you need to go underneath the hillslopes.

"This is where we take the manual measurements," explains Luke while standing under one of the hillslopes. From down here it looks like the underside of a steel bridge or highway ramp. Things are still a bit drippy from the rain, too. A small puddle on the concrete floor reflects a blue sky crisscrossed with white triangles. Coils of cables and tubing hang from the green steel beams. And there are lots of plastic syringes.

## "LEO provides a tool unlike any other in the world to test the models that we use to make predictions about climate change."

"These are suction lysimeters," says Luke. Clear tubing connected to the end of each syringe goes to a water sampler buried in the dirt. Pulling the plunger draws out water, which is then analyzed. Scientists take samples of gases using the lysimeters, too. It all depends on what they're studying. "We have four hundred ninety-six different locations in the soil," says Luke. "So we decide which depths and which locations along the hillslope we want to sample." Think about tracking a chemical spill. How far and how fast does the toxic stuff move though a watershed? How long do cleanup crews have before it reaches a stream or river? LEO can run experiments to find out by adding traceable markers to the water and tracking their path and speed.

Taking water samples is part of mapping the evolution of soil, too. Carbon levels in the samples tell scientists that the

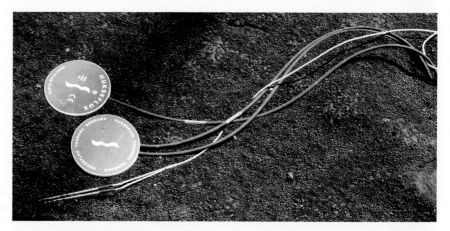

Sensors like these are buried in the soil of LEO's three hillslopes to measure soil moisture, water flow, and gases.

volcanic rock is breaking down into soil. Why? Rain makes carbonic acid as it soaks up carbon dioxide while falling through the air. Carbonic acid in rain is what wears away grave markers and stone statues over time. The mild acid also eats away at LEO's volcanic rock. "It's an indicator of how much the soil is weathering," explains Luke. "So in part we will be observing how the hillslope changes and in part we will be manipulating the climate on the hillslope." The weather and atmosphere inside LEO is controllable, providing "a broader range of climatic conditions than you could get if you put some instruments in the field and just waited to see what nature gives you," explains Luke. LEO scientists can create short bursts of heavy rain or long-lasting light rain and compare erosion. The hillslopes will be planted in a few years. Once plant communities are growing, the scientists can create droughts or downpours and see how different plants' roots deal with it.

These are answers needed to plan for what's coming. "We want to know, if the climate's different in the future, how is it going to change the water we rely on?" says Luke. Will more

Luke Pangle checks the lysimeters underneath one of LEO's three identical artificial hillslopes.

Luke takes a ride in LEO's cable-suspended personal transporter, or gantry. Once seeds are planted, no one will walk on the soil.

water evaporate from soil and not make it into rivers? Will erosion increase or decrease? Will plants with deep roots or shallow roots do better? "LEO provides a tool unlike any other in the world to test the models that we use to make predictions about climate change," says Luke. Climate change predictions come from computer programs, called models, which simulate what will happen over time. "And LEO is a really exceptional tool to rigorously test those models and make sure they're accurate predictions."

Climate models are only as good as the information that goes into them. Models are made up of sets of equations that represent rates of evaporation and runoff, root absorption and rainfall amounts. Hydrology equations usually come from small lab experiments, and results from these don't necessarily hold up on a larger scale. Just because it takes one liter of water one hour to soak through one meter of sand doesn't mean it takes an equal amount of time for 100 liters to get through 100 meters of sand. At LEO they can test on a real-world-sized hillslope. Luke says that when they do experiments they start with the newest computer model, get its prediction for LEO, run the actual experiment, and see what really happens. "And then we go back and see if the model was right or wrong, and if it was wrong, why," he explains.

A good example is one of the first experiments done at LEO. It measured how long it took for the amount of water running off the hillslope watershed to equal the amount of rain falling on it. The model predicted twenty-two hours of rain for LEO to reach this equilibrium. "It was completely wrong," says Luke. It happened a lot quicker and ended up eroding out a gully down the hillslope's center. "That model is an example of the type of model that might be used to predict

how water flows through the landscape under different climate conditions," says Luke. Climate conditions that we need to be able to predict, such as how rainfall patterns change and affect fertile crop soil or how pollutants move through underground water. It's why LEO is so important right now, when our climate is changing. "We stand to learn a lot here that we couldn't learn as quickly or perhaps at all by doing just field studies," says Luke. "So that's why I'm here."

# FLASH-BACK
# TO THE BIOSPHERIANS

The biospherians grew food in the half-acre agricultural area. Some plants did better than others and the hungry residents were eager to plant what produced the most food. This meant eating lots of calorie-dense sweet potatoes. Jane Poynter wrote that they ate so many of the orange tubers that their skin turned yellow.

The Technosphere is Biosphere 2's gigantic heating, ventilation, and air conditioning (HVAC) system. "And we're walking through the ductwork right now," says Nate Allen. "We can look up and see the heating and cooling grates that go up into the biomes."

# CHAPTER 5

# SUSTAINABLE CITY

**W**atch your head here," says a bearded man in blue jeans and a white button-down shirt. Nate Allen taps the top edge of the hatch door as he steps through, his fingers brushing a red-lettered sign. It reads SAVANNAH AIRLOCK, but no grassy plain is in sight, nor anything else living. Nate is surrounded by dimly lit passageways with walls of steel and concrete that wind past water tanks and metal cabinets full of switches and wires connected by endless electrical and computer cables. Rows of white water pipes as thick as coffee cans run along the ceiling overhead and up and down walls, too. The hum of droning machines and rushing air echoes about. The air lock we just walked through leads to what's beneath the biome, the savannah's power and plumbing systems. Welcome to Biosphere 2's basement.

"This is called the Technosphere," says Nate Allen. Earth's atmo*sphere* is where cold rain and warm winds come from. "But Biosphere 2's weather is produced by *techno*logy." The biospherians combined *techno*- with -*sphere* to get the name. The Technosphere fills two underground acres with weather-making machinery. It features twenty-six floor-to-ceiling steel chambers called air handlers. They deliver air that's climate-

"At the other end of each one of these wires is a sensor that controls how we maintain temperature, humidity, and all the other environmental conditions inside," explains Nate Allen.

controlled to order into each of the glassed-in ecosystems above. Networks of sensors and valves monitor and control the temperature, humidity, and other environmental conditions inside the three-acre greenhouse.

The Technosphere goes pretty much unnoticed by the tourists upstairs, much like most infrastructure that supports our lives. We depend on electricity and water in our homes and schools, but don't think much about them (at least until

Biosphere 2's Technosphere has cabinets full of switches and wires that create weather for each biome.

the power goes out or the faucet runs dry). Nate Allen wants to change that. He'd like people to understand where our electricity comes from and who decides how much water we can use. It's going to matter more and more in the coming century. Demand for resources to run the technology and households of our growing human population is on the rise. Can we keep making more energy without harming the planet? How can towns use water and other natural resources more efficiently so we don't run out? "This is a big challenge," says Nate.

# There's no time to waste, says Nate. "Climate change is here."

As Biosphere 2's sustainability coordinator, that challenge is his job. "For cities, sustainability really means *How do you use electricity and water?*" He's studying just that by experimenting on a mini-city—Biosphere 2. It's called the Model City program.

Biosphere 2 is more than the rainforest, ocean, and other ecosystems. The glass-covered structure and its Technosphere are part of a 34-acre (14-hectare) campus. It includes dormitories, meeting rooms, offices, a visitor center and café, a power regulating plant, and a wastewater treatment facility. Just like any city, Biosphere 2 supplies water and power to keep things going. Nate Allen's Model City program uses the entire campus as a laboratory. The program researches and tests green technologies and methods that conserve energy and water. What's being learned makes the campus more sustainable, educates the public, and shows other cities what's possible. It also lowers Biosphere 2's big utility bills.

Nate Allen studied geology and environmental education before coming to work at Biosphere 2 as its sustainability coordinator.

The Model City program uses Biosphere 2's entire 34-acre (14-hectare) campus as a laboratory for water and energy conservation.

This solar test bed is a hill with solar panels sitting atop different ground covers. Nate Allen compared the amounts of electricity they made over time.

## SOLAR TURF

Solar energy is one project. A hillside across from the glass pyramid at Biosphere 2 is covered in photovoltaic panels, those flat rectangular solar panels that make electricity. The hillside panels aren't sitting on dirt; the ground under them is covered up. Part of the hill has green artificial turf beneath the panels. Other panels on the hillside test beds sit on top of heavy white plastic. Does what's under the solar panels matter? To find out, Nate compared how much electricity each test bed made. The winner was artificial turf. It keeps the solar panels working while not overheating in the harsh desert sun. Does this mean people should put artificial turf under their rooftop solar panels? Not necessarily. But there are lots of artificial hills in the Southwest that need covering up. Metal mining operations create mountains of leftover dusty rubble. What if they could

Biosphere 2 needs to run only half of its twenty-six air handlers at once to provide weather to the ecosystems upstairs. The biospherians made sure they had lots of backup systems.

The sunny desert surrounding Biosphere 2 seems perfect for solar energy, but overheated photovoltaic panels can't make as much electricity.

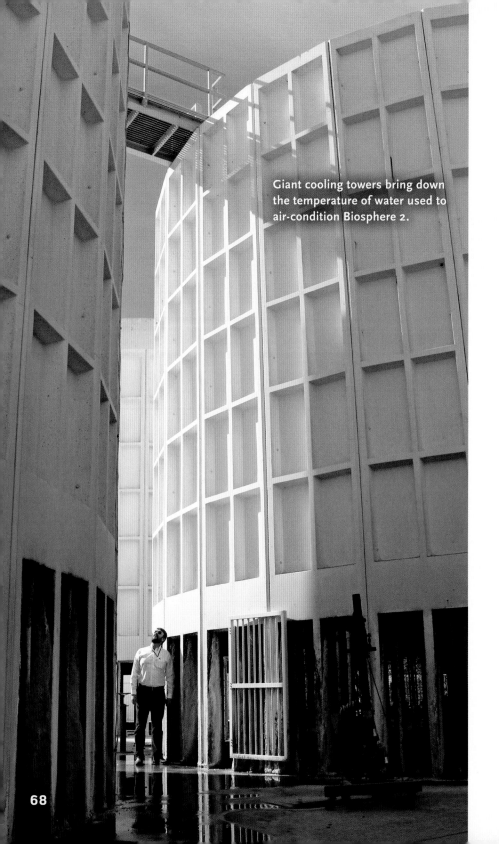

Giant cooling towers bring down the temperature of water used to air-condition Biosphere 2.

be put to work making electricity with solar panels? Now mining companies know what kind of covering works best under photovoltaic panels.

The solar test bed project is a good example of why Nate finds working at Biosphere 2 so fascinating. He likes solving real-world problems while doing science. "I don't just have to study solar cells in order to do solar research," Nate explains. He also gets to study covering materials, kinds of wiring systems, the effects of weather, and other parts of a whole system. Nate is better able to help the people who put the technology to work in the real world because of it. Knowing what works best from the get-go saves time, which saves energy and resources and gets us to sustainability sooner.

### SMARTER ENERGY

New technologies only help if they're used in a smart way. Using solar, wind, and other kinds of renewable energy is great. But renewables require new methods of energy usage too, says Nate. You can burn fossil fuels, like coal or natural gas, whenever you need to. During winter, a power plant makes extra electricity to heat homes by burning more fuel. The demand for power determines the supply of fossil fuel needed. "With renewables, supply has to inform demand," explains Nate. It's reversed because weather affects renewable energy. Solar panels don't work without sunshine. Storing electricity for later takes lots of expensive batteries. It's more efficient to use solar energy while the sun is making it. The trick is to synchronize the power demand and the sunshine supply. At Biosphere 2 they're testing out this idea by using their solar energy to run electric water pumps. A half million gallons

(2 million liters) of well water are stored in tanks onsite, so pumps are big electricity users at Biosphere 2. "Can we pump enough water during the day when the sun is out to meet our water demand?" asks Nate. If so, the pumps can be turned off at night instead of running on power from fossil fuels.

Better planning can make all kinds of energy systems more efficient. Pumping water when the sun's out is just one example. Another is using computers that predict weather, or smart apps that know how people live to save energy used to heat and cool buildings. Heating systems that know a cold snap is coming can warm things up to prepare. Likewise, a thermostat that knows when you'll be home on a hot day can slowly

is used to heat and cool the air inside Biosphere 2. It
in the energy plant where some water is heated to 200°F
and other water is chilled down to 40°F (4°C). Thick
shuttle the water into the Technosphere, where air han-
use it to warm or cool the air going into the ecosystems.

The reddish tank at Nate's back holds water collected off the roofs of Biosphere 2's casita dormitories.

and efficiently cool the house before you get there. Smarter technology can save energy.

## HARVESTING RAIN

Nate stands near a low pinkish-beige building on Biosphere 2's campus. Behind him are cacti-covered rocky hills. "Here in the desert Southwest, we need to use water in the most efficient way possible," he says. Saving water is the other big part of Biosphere 2's Model City program. Nate points toward a row of small planted saplings lined up near the low building. "This experiment is about how we take advantage of a really important resource," explains Nate. "The water that falls out of the sky as rain." Black pipes create paths to every tree from a metal tub under the building's gutter downspout. Each of the young trees sits alongside a bowl-shaped shallow hole, called a catchment basin. Its job is to funnel every drop of water that comes its way. Some of the rainwater catchment basins are mulched with leaves or gravel. This experiment is testing the ground-covering mulches. "We're interested to see the effect of those different kinds of ground covers on the performance of the plants and the overall soil moisture over time," explains Nate.

Using mulch that soaks up the most rain possible makes a difference in the desert. Half of all city water in Tucson, Arizona, goes to watering gardens and trees. Businesses there are required to collect rainwater for at least 50 percent of their landscaping water instead of using treated city water. Harvesting rainwater that runs off roofs for watering plants goes on all over the Southwest, including at Biosphere 2. But is that water really safe to use, especially on vegetables that

Nate Allen checks the mulch of the catchment basin that funnels water to a mesquite sapling. When it rains, water fills the metal tanks, which shuttle water to each young tree.

Biosphere 2 researchers, such as Luke Pangle, are helping to prepare us for global climate change.

people will eat? A citizen science project that Nate is helping with aims to find out. The project is testing water quality in five hundred rainwater tanks in Tucson. The findings are helping rainwater harvesters collect cleaner water by using screens to keep out bugs and leaves so bacteria doesn't grow. Choosing tanks made of lightproof material keeps algae out, too.

Besides harvesting rainwater, Biosphere 2 also uses lots of environmentally friendly materials in their buildings, such as recycled concrete, energy-saving windows, and solar-powered hot water. Information panels all around the Biosphere 2 campus explain how the rain-gathering techniques and energy-saving technologies work. It's all part of being a Model City for a greener twenty-first century.

## EARTH FIRST

There's no time to waste, says Nate. "Climate change is here." Biosphere 2 aims and aspires to educate the public about sustainability, especially in the Southwest. Arizonans aren't strangers to drought. Battles over the water rights to rivers and underground water are old news out West. Curious tourists coming to see where the biospherians ate and slept often leave knowing a bit about harvesting rainwater and solar panels. That's a good thing.

Meanwhile, scientists working at Biosphere 2 are tackling the science side of climate change. It's part of why the University of Arizona's B2 Earthscience program runs the one-of-a-kind research facility. Biosphere 2 scientists are using the giant greenhouse to track how the climate is changing, predict what will happen, and figure out ways to prepare for a new kind of future. The real-world scale of the huge glass-

covered laboratory can help them study how a warmed-up world affects our oceans, forests, water resources, and landscapes. Will rainforests adapt to higher temperatures? Can ocean life withstand more acidic seas? Could drenching rainstorms change how soil is made? The visitors who walk through Biosphere 2's famous metal air-lock hatch also discover something about the science going on there now. That's a pretty awesome thing. Biosphere 2 might have been built for living on Mars, but its current mission is to help plan for Earth's near future.

## FLASH-BACK TO THE BIOSPHERIANS

Roy Walford and Mark Nelson talk business in Mission Control during their 1991–93 mission. The large room was the computer-filled command center and meeting space. The matching jumpsuit uniforms were worn only for official events. Each biospherian had one in red and one in blue.

## A HEARTFELT THANK-YOU

This book would not have been possible without the enthusiastic cooperation of the scientists and staff at the University of Arizona's B2 Earthscience facility at Biosphere 2. Thank you for taking the time and having the patience to allow us to tag along, take photos, and ask endless questions. First and foremost among them is Kevin Bonine, who set this project in motion and to whom we are most grateful. We would also like to acknowledge the generous support of the B2 deputy director John Adams and Peter Troch, science director. Sincere thanks are owed to the biogeochemist extraordinaire Joost van Haren for showing us his work in the rainforest, and to the marine ecologist Rafe Sagarin for sharing his vision of the B2 ocean. The science behind the Landscape Evolution Observatory would have been incomprehensible without the invaluable help of the hydrologist Luke Pangle. We'd also like to thank Rebecca Minor for giving us a tour of the Mount Bigelow site, and Nate Allen for showing us the wonders that lie in the basement under Biosphere 2. We also appreciate the help of the original biospherian Jane Poynter, who provided a number of historical photographs. A long-overdue recognition goes to our good friends Tonya and David Herron, who continually welcome our pup, Ruby, into their home when we're off tracking down scientists. And last but by no means least, we're ever indebted to our editor, Erica Zappy Wainer, for making us a veteran Scientists in the Field team. Thanks, y'all!

—Tom & Mary Kay

## WORDS TO KNOW

**algae**—simple plantlike living things that mostly live in water and photosynthesize their own food.

**anemometer**—an instrument for measuring wind speed.

**biodiverse**—having a wide variety of species of animals and plants in an environment.

**biome**—a major type of natural community of plants and animals, usually defined by geography and climate conditions.

**biosphere**—the region surrounding Earth between rock and sky that can support life.

**calcium carbonate**—a solid form of calcium found in nature as limestone and marble and in bones and shells.

**carbon dioxide**—a colorless, odorless gas in the atmosphere made of two oxygen atoms and one carbon atom, $CO_2$, which forms when fossil fuels are burned. It is also exhaled by animals and absorbed by plants during photosynthesis.

**carbonic acid**—an acid made when carbon dioxide is dissolved in water.

**climate change**—the rise in the average temperature of Earth's atmosphere and oceans since the late nineteenth century; global warming.

**closed system**—a region that is isolated or separated from its surroundings and does not exchange any matter or interact with said surroundings.

**coral**—small backboneless sea animals that live in colonies, whose skeletons create stony reefs.

**ecosystem**—a system made up of a group of living things, its environment, and the relationships between them.

**El Niño**—a period of months or years when temperatures are unusually warm in the central and eastern Pacific ocean near the equator.

**erosion**—the wearing away of rock or soil from water, wind, ice, etc.

**fossil fuels**—a burnable, energy-full material such as coal, petroleum, and natural gas that formed from once living things.

**geologist**—a scientist who studies Earth's crust of rock.

**hydrologist**—a scientist who studies water and how it circulates between the land and the atmosphere.

**hygrometer**—an instrument for measuring the amount of moisture or humidity in the air.

**lidar**—a light detection and ranging device; a radar that uses lasers instead of radio waves to create maps and images.

**lysimeter**—an instrument for collecting water from soil so that the amounts of dissolved matter can be measured.

**marine biology**—the study of ocean life.

**model**—a computer simulation based on mathematical equations and entered data.

**ocean acidification**—the current lowering in the pH of the Earth's oceans due to the increased levels of carbon dioxide in the atmosphere.

**photosynthesis**—the way plants make food from water, carbon dioxide in the air, and sunlight.

**photovoltaic**—technology that creates an electric current from light, like a solar panel.

**precipitation**—water falling from clouds, such as rain, snow, sleet, ice, or hail.

**primates**—a member of the the group of mammals that includes humans, monkeys, apes, and lemurs.

**rainforest**—a dense forest with heavy rainfall most of the year.

**renewable energy**—energy from a source that doesn't get used up, such as wind or solar power.

**soil**—the top layer of the ground, made up of rock, minerals, and animal and plant matter.

**sustainability**—the ability of something to last or keep going for a long time; using methods that do not completely use up or destroy natural resources.

**variable**—something that can change, be changed, or varies in an experiment.

**VOCs**—volatile organic compounds; unstable chemicals that readily vaporize into the air and easily react with other gases.

**water cycle**—the cycle of water moving between land and air as it evaporates from oceans and lakes, forms clouds, and returns to Earth as rain and snow; hydrologic cycle.

**watershed**—all the land area that drains into a particular body of water, like a river, lake, or sea.

**weathering**—the processes that break down rock exposed to water and weather.

# FIND OUT MORE!

### Biosphere 2

Want to find out more about what's going on at Biosphere 2? Their website is a great place to start. You can take a virtual tour or find out how to visit in person. The website features lots of videos and photos of LEO, the B2 ocean, and news updates on projects, too. Go to b2science.org.

**Guided (Virtual) Tour:** b2science.org/visitor/campus/guidetour

**Rainforest:** b2science.org/earth/facility/biome-rainforest

**Desert Sea:** b2science.org/ocean

**Landscape Evolution Observatory:** b2science.org/leo

**Model City:** b2science.org/institute/modelcity

**Twitter:** @B2science

**Facebook:** www.facebook.com/Biosphere2

### The Water Cycle

Everything you've ever wanted to know about where rain comes from and where groundwater goes can be found on the U.S. Geological Survey's website. There's also a terrific interactive diagram in three levels and a dozen languages. Go to water.usgs.gov/edu/watercycle-kids.html.

### Climate Change and Modeling

The Center for Science Education has terrific information on climate change evidence and impacts. Go to scied.ucar.edu/climate.

The Environmental Protection Agency has an information-filled climate change website for young people, too. Go to www.epa.gov/climatechange/kids.

The National Academy of Sciences website "Climate Modeling 101" explains how scientists use computers to model the future climate so we know what's on the way. Go to nas-sites.org/climatemodeling.

### The Biospherians

Curious about the original biospherians and their two-year mission? A number of them have written books about their experiences. They are listed under Chapter 1's selected bibliography on page 77. The website for the group that built Biosphere 2 also has some information. Go to www.biospherics.org/biosphere2.

# QUOTE SOURCES & SELECTED BIBLIOGRAPHY BY CHAPTER

## 1. Spaceship Earth

All quotes from Dr. John Adams, deputy director of Biosphere 2, are from voice-recorded interviews made in January 2014, onsite at Biosphere 2 in Oracle, Arizona.

"After thirteen months in Biosphere 2, we were starving . . .": Poynter, p. 245.

Alling, Abigail, Mark Nelson, and Sally Silverstone. *Life Under Glass: The Inside Story of Biosphere 2.* Santa Fe, N.M.: Synergetic Press, 1993.

Allen, John. *Biosphere 2: The Human Experiment.* New York: Viking, 1991.

B2 Science. "History, Timeline, Fast Facts." b2science.org/who/history.

Lew, Julie. "Peering into a World Under Glass." *New York Times,* December 22, 1991.

O'Callaghan, Tiffany. "A Biosphere Reborn." *New Scientist* 219, no. 2927 (July 27–August 2, 2013): 41.

Poynter, Jane. *The Human Experiment: Two Years and Twenty Minutes Inside Biosphere 2.* New York: Thunder's Mouth Press, 2006.

Reider, Rebecca. *Dreaming the Biosphere: The Theater of All Possibilities.* Albuquerque, N.M.: University of New Mexico Press, 2009.

## 2. Experimental Rainforest

All quotes from the biogeochemist Dr. Joost van Haren, assistant research professor, Biosphere 2, are from interviews with the author voice-recorded in January and March of 2014, onsite at Biosphere 2 in Oracle, Arizona, and were reviewed by the scientist.

Pegoraro, E., A. Rey, L. Abrell, J. Van Haren, and G. Lin. "Drought Effect on Isoprene Production and Consumption in Biosphere 2 Tropical Rainforest." *Global Change Biology* 12 (2006): 456–69.

Rainforest Biome. b2science.org/earth/facility/biome-rainforest.

van Haren, J. L. M., et al. "Do Plant Species Influence Soil $CO_2$ and $N_2O$ Fluxes in a Diverse Tropical Forest?" *Journal of Geophysical Research-Biogeosciences* 115, no. G3 (September 2010): 1–9.

## 3. Ocean with Desert Dreams

All quotes from Dr. Rafe Sagarin, marine ecologist at the University of Arizona's Biosphere 2, are from interviews with the author voice-recorded in January of 2014, onsite at Biosphere 2 in Oracle, Arizona, and were reviewed by the scientist.

Augustowska, Anna. "Biosphere 2 Plans to Build Small Replica of Gulf of California." Arizona Public Media, April 15, 2014. www.azpm.org/s/18448-biosphere-2-plans-to-build-small-replica-of-gulf-of-california.

Beal, Tom. "UA Scientist Awarded $1M to Research Ocean Viruses." *Arizona Daily Star,* December 4, 2012.

Biosphere 2. "A Story of Two Oceans: Biosphere 2 and the Gulf of California." Viewing gallery exhibit at Biosphere 2, Oracle, Arizona.

B2 Science. "Ocean Biome." b2science.org/earth/facility/biome-ocean.

———. "The Desert Sea at Biosphere 2: Transforming the Ocean." vimeo.com/88325332.

NOAA Pacific Marine Environmental Laboratory. "Ocean Acidification: The Other Carbon Dioxide Problem." www.pmel.noaa.gov/co2/story/Ocean+Acidification.

UA: Institute of the Environment. "Rafe Sagarin." www.environment.arizona.edu/rafe-sagarin.

## 4. Earth Science Observatory

All quotes from Dr. Luke Pangle, postdoctoral research associate at Biosphere 2, are from voice-recorded interviews with the author in January and March of 2014 onsite at Biosphere 2 in Oracle, Arizona, and were reviewed by the scientist. Quotes from Rebecca Minor, research specialist at University of Arizona's B2 Earthscience, are from interviews with the author en route to and at the Mount Bigelow site in Coronado National Forest, Mount Lemmon, Arizona, and were reviewed by her as well.

"Artificial Watershed Provides 'Real' Data." *USA Today* magazine 141, no. 2811 (December 2012): 3–4.

Beal, Tom. "New Observatory at Biosphere 2 Offers a Look at Life's Thin Veneer." *Arizona Daily Star,* December 3, 2012.

Biosphere 2. "What Is LEO?" Exhibit in Biosphere 2's human habitat, Oracle, Arizona.

B2 Science. "LEO: Landscape Evolution Observatory." b2science.org/leo.

Powledge, Fred. "Biosphere II Is Back: The Perfect Intermediary between Nature and Lab." *BioScience* 62, no. 9 (September 2012): 790–95.

Reed, Shipherd, and Ruben Ruiz. "The Story of LEO." youtu.be/dzvgmDbrgxU.

Verrilli, Austen. "Biosphere 2 Observatory Turns Planetary Clock Back to Zero to Study Surface Changes." *Environmental Monitor,* November 25, 2013. www.fondriest.com/news/land-evolution-observatory-biosphere-2.htm.

## 5. Sustainable City

All quotes from the Biosphere 2 staff scientist Nate Allen are from interviews with the author voice-recorded in January 2014, onsite at Biosphere 2 in Oracle, Arizona, except "This is a big challenge . . ." and "At the other end . . ." (caption), which are from B2 Science, "Biosphere 2 Model City Program."

Beal, Tom. "UA Looks at Mine-Waste Piles, Sees Potential Solar-Power Site." *Arizona Daily Star,* July 18, 2010.

B2 Science. "Biosphere 2 as a Model City for Simulating and Demonstration of Innovative Energy and Water Management Strategies." b2science.org/earth/research/energy-model.

B2 Science. "Biosphere 2 Model City Program." July 27, 2012. youtu.be/y4eHYmlMLqI.

B2 Science. "Energy & Sustainability." b2science.org/earth/research/energy.

de Dios, John. "Biosphere 2: A Model City for Sustainability." *Tucson Weekly,* November 13, 2011.

# INDEX

# SCIENTISTS IN THE FIELD
## Where Science Meets Adventure

Check out these titles to meet more scientists who are out in the field—
and contributing every day to our knowledge of the world around us:

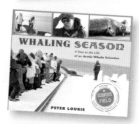

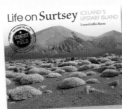

Looking for even more adventure? Craving updates on the work of your favorite scientists, as well as in-depth video
footage, audio, photography, and more? Then visit the new Scientists in the Field website!

## sciencemeetsadventure.com